WHAT'S INSIDE A Remote-Controlled Car?

ARNOLD RINGSTAD

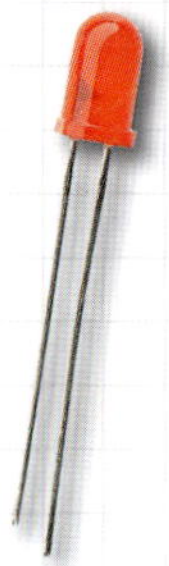

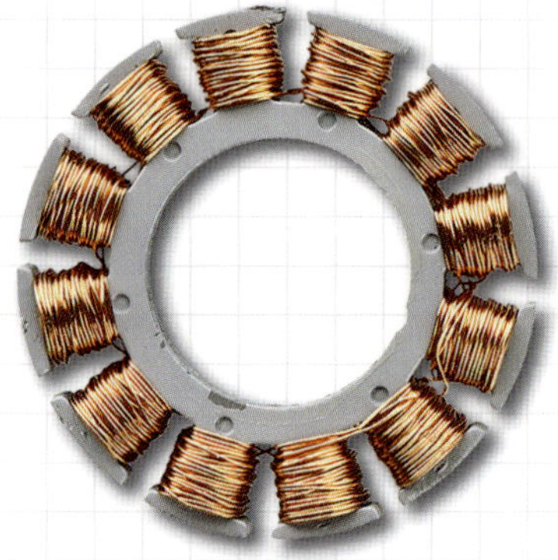

The Child's World
childsworld.com

Published by The Child's World®
1980 Lookout Drive • Mankato, MN 56003-1705
800-599-READ • www.childsworld.com

Photographs ©: Rick Orndorf, cover (car), 1 (car), 4, 7, 9, 11, 13, 14, 17 (antenna), 19, 24; Pavel Mikushin/ Shutterstock Images, cover (battery), 1 (battery), 8, 15 (battery), 20, 22 (battery); Shutterstock Images, cover (motor), 1 (motor), 2, 3 (plug), 3 (circuit board), 5 (glasses), 6, 10 (spring), 12, 15 (component), 17 (circuit board), 18, 21, 22 (component), 23 (motor); Praiwun Thungsarn/Shutterstock Images, 3 (screwdriver), 5 (screwdriver), 10 (screwdriver), 16, 23 (screwdriver); Shyripa Alexandr/Shutterstock Images, 5 (gloves)

ISBN 9781503832053
LCCN 2018962809

Printed in the United States of America
PA02419

About the Author

Arnold Ringstad lives in Minnesota.

He enjoys racing remote-controlled cars.

Contents

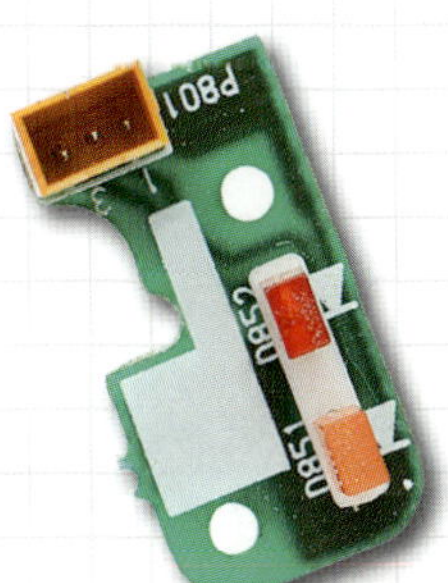

Materials and Safety

Materials

- [ ] Phillips screwdriver
- [ ] Remote-controlled car
- [ ] Safety glasses
- [ ] Work gloves

Safety

- Never try to open a battery.
- Always be careful with sharp objects, such as screwdrivers.
- Wear work gloves to protect your hands from sharp edges.
- Wear safety glasses in case pieces snap off.

Remote-controlled car

Important!

Be sure to get an adult's permission before taking anything apart. When you're taking things apart, have an adult nearby in case you need help or have questions.

Inside a Remote-Controlled Car

Many people enjoy using remote-controlled cars. Some people like to race them. Others drive them just for fun. How does a remote-controlled car work? What's inside?

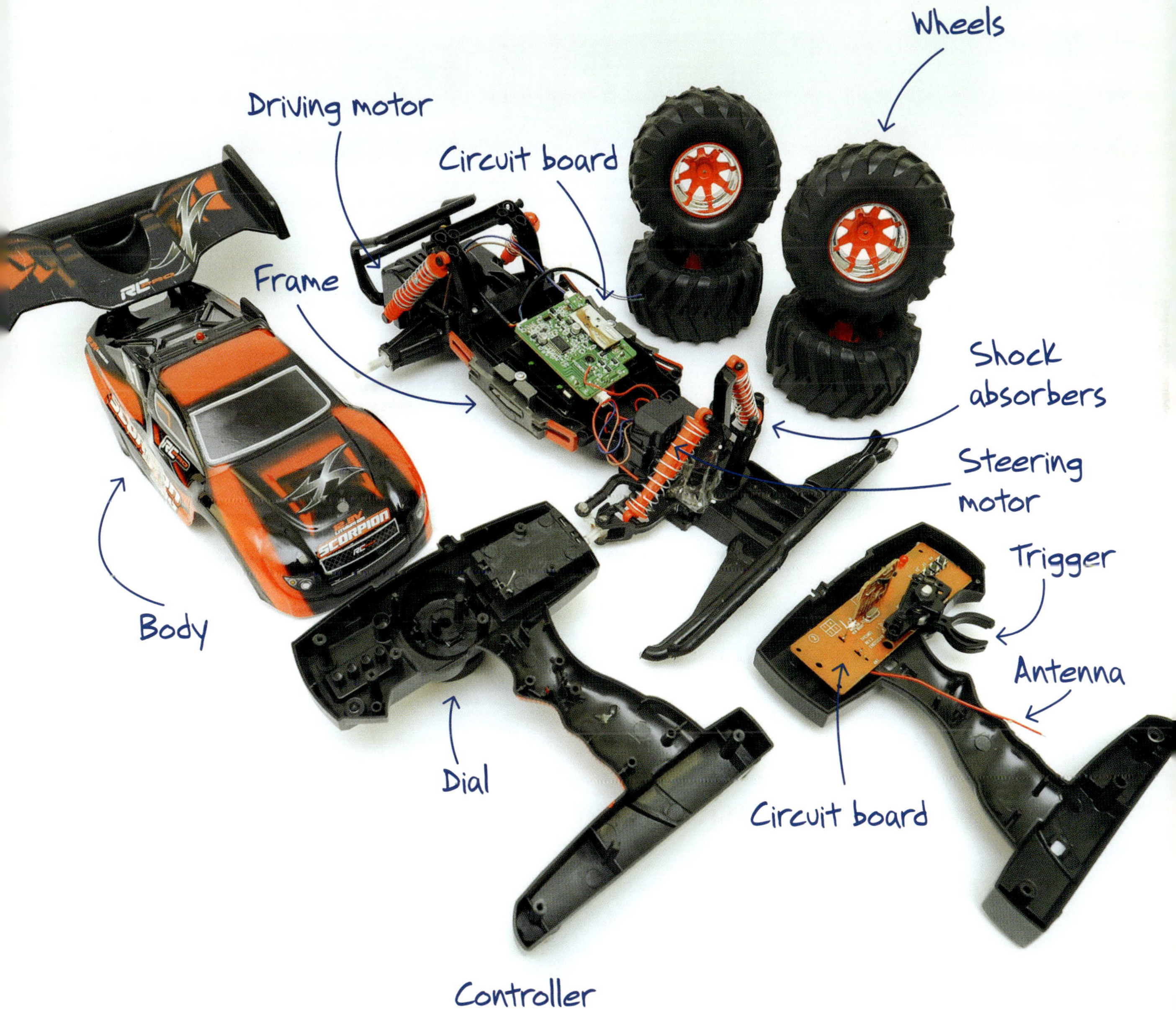
Wheels
Driving motor
Circuit board
Frame
Shock absorbers
Steering motor
Trigger
Antenna
Body
Dial
Circuit board
Controller

Opening the Remote-Controlled Car

First, flip over the car and take out the battery. You may have to unscrew the battery cover. Next, pull the car's plastic body off the frame. Now you can see the **circuit board** and the **motors**.

Safety Note

Never try to open a battery. There are dangerous chemicals inside.

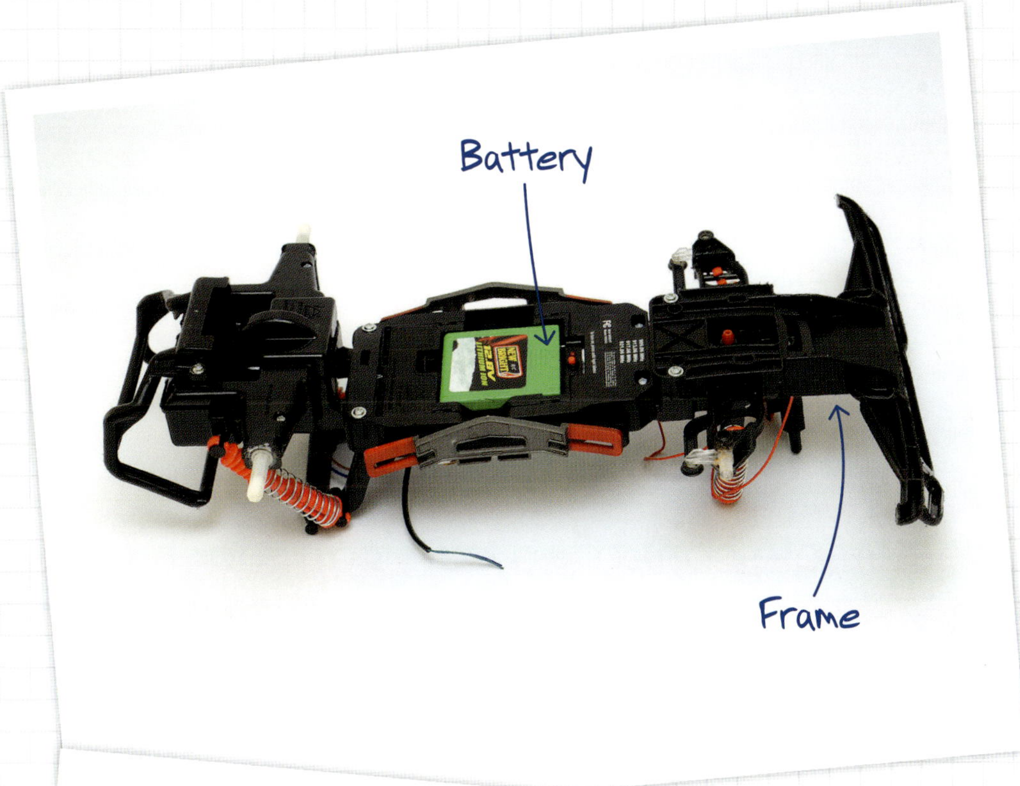
Battery
Frame

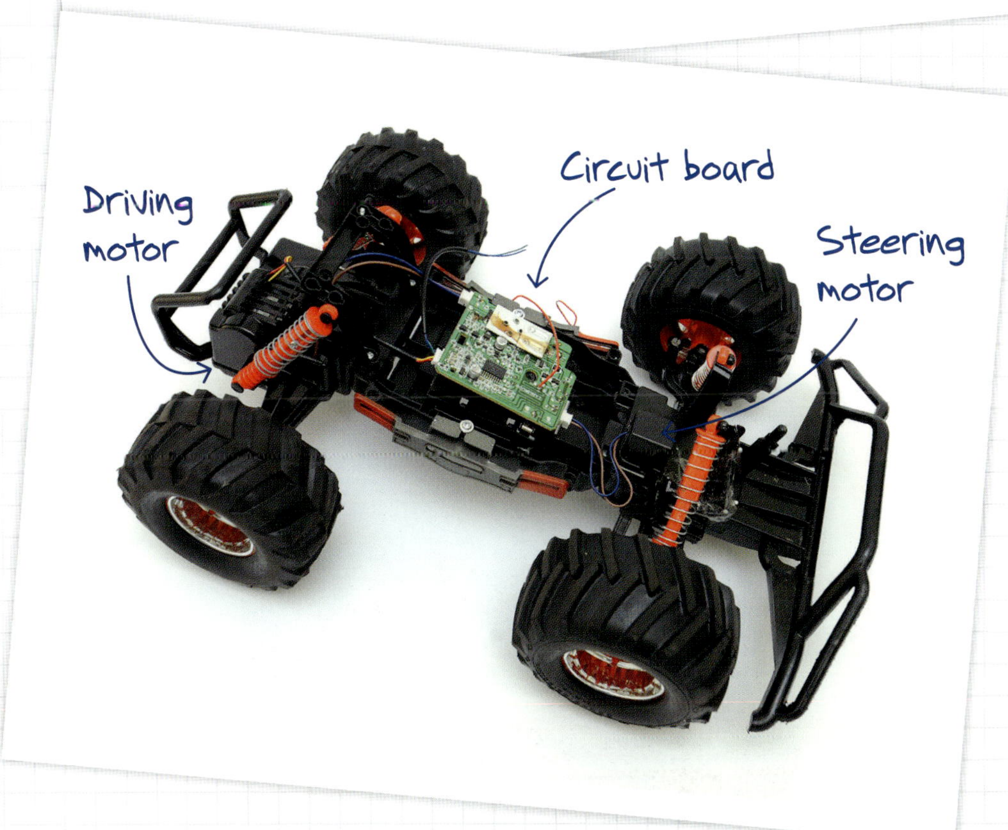
Driving motor
Circuit board
Steering motor

Protecting the Car

Remote-controlled cars can reach high speeds. But the parts inside are **delicate**. Bumpers in the front and back protect the car in case of a crash. Shock absorbers keep the wheels steady on rough surfaces.

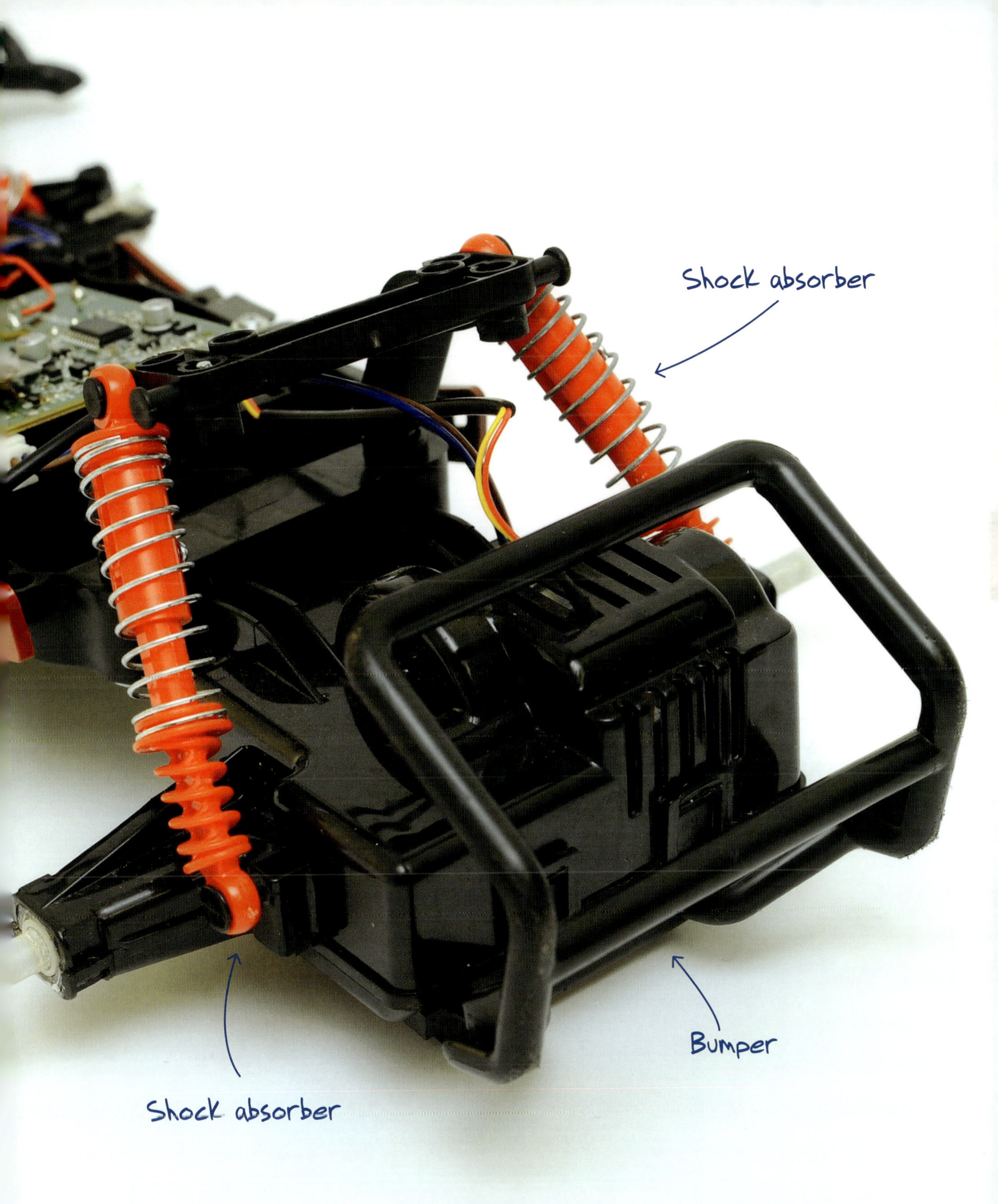
Shock absorber
Bumper
Shock absorber

Opening the Remote

Next, open the remote. Find the screws holding the remote together. Unscrew them and pull the sides apart. Inside you can see the remote's circuit board.

Safety Note

Circuit boards may have sharp edges. Be careful when handling them.

Circuit board

Sending Signals

To drive a remote-controlled car, a person uses the remote. The remote has a trigger and a dial.

The trigger controls the car's speed.

Safety Note

Some parts, such as the antenna, may have exposed sharp wires. Be careful when handling them.

The trigger tells the car to move forward or backward. The dial tells the car to turn. When you move these parts, the circuit board creates a **radio signal**. It sends out the signal using the **antenna**.

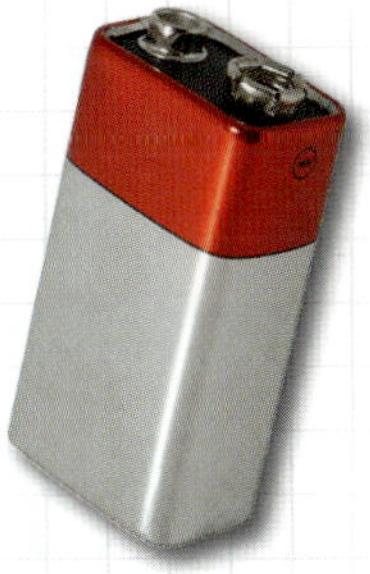

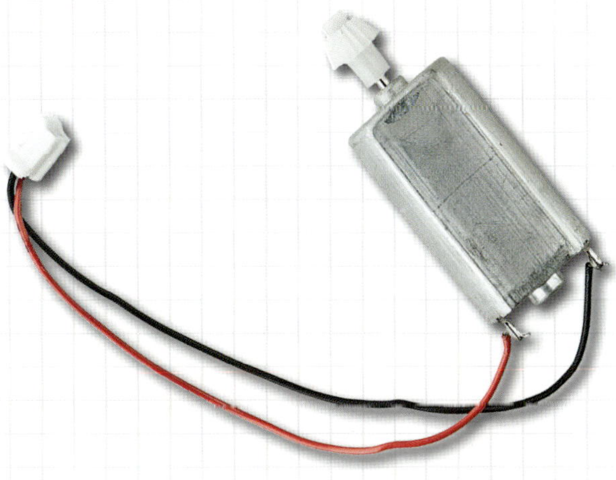

Receiving Signals

An antenna on the car's circuit board receives the signal. The circuit board is connected to the battery and motors. It gets power from the battery. Then it sends power to the motors.

The motor in the front makes the front wheels turn left and right. The remote's dial controls this motor.

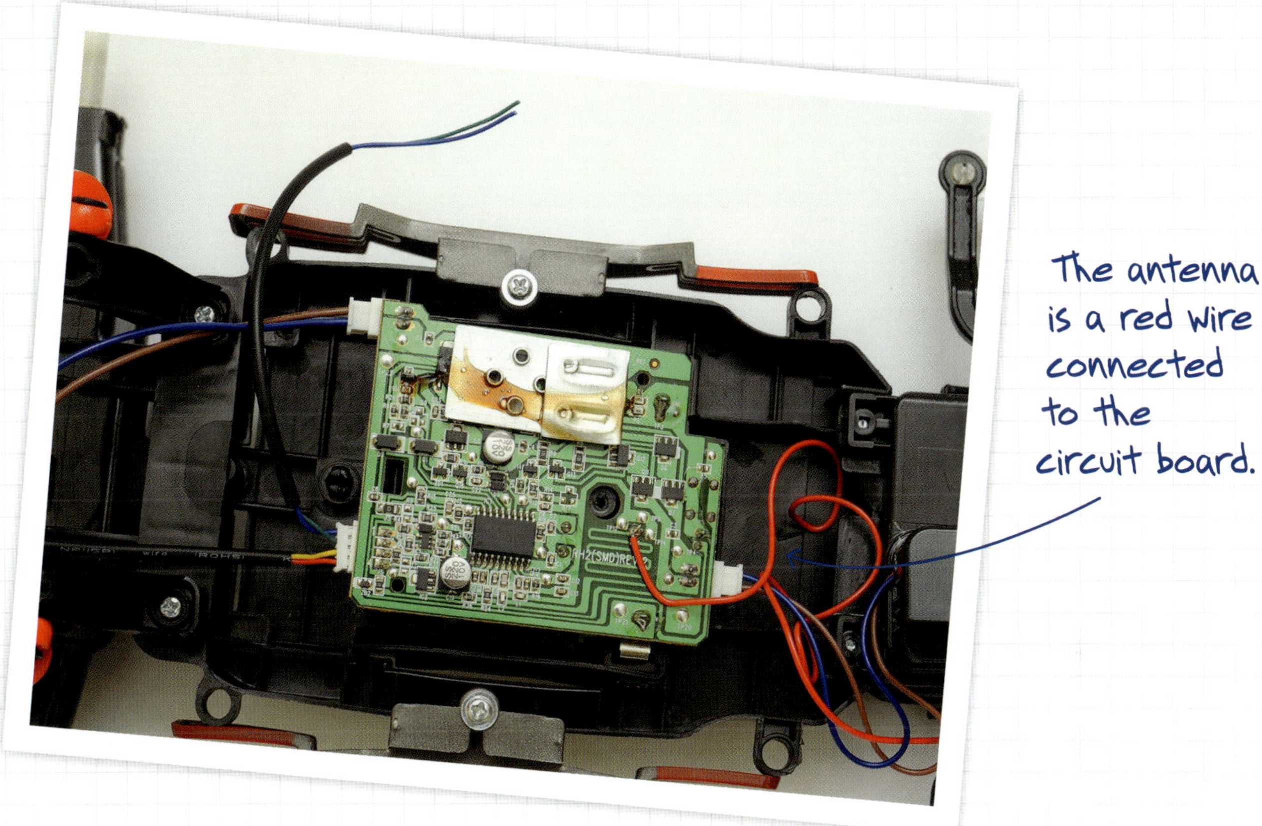

The motor in the back makes the back wheels drive forward. The remote's trigger controls this motor.

Time to Drive

Together, the motors allow the car to drive. It can zoom around tight corners. It can speed along in a straight line. Or it can spin around in circles. The car can keep driving until the battery runs out of power. Then, the battery must be plugged in to recharge.

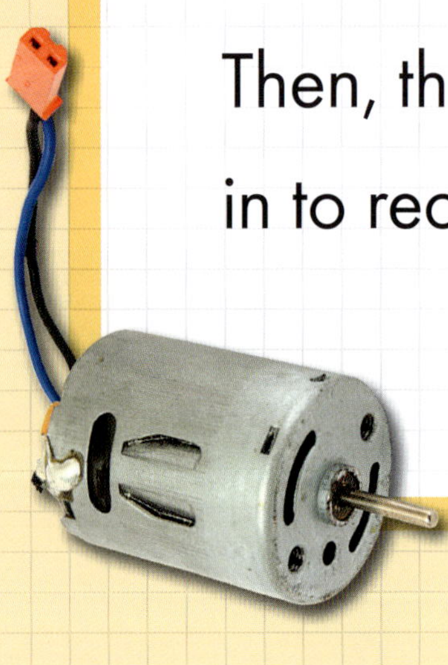

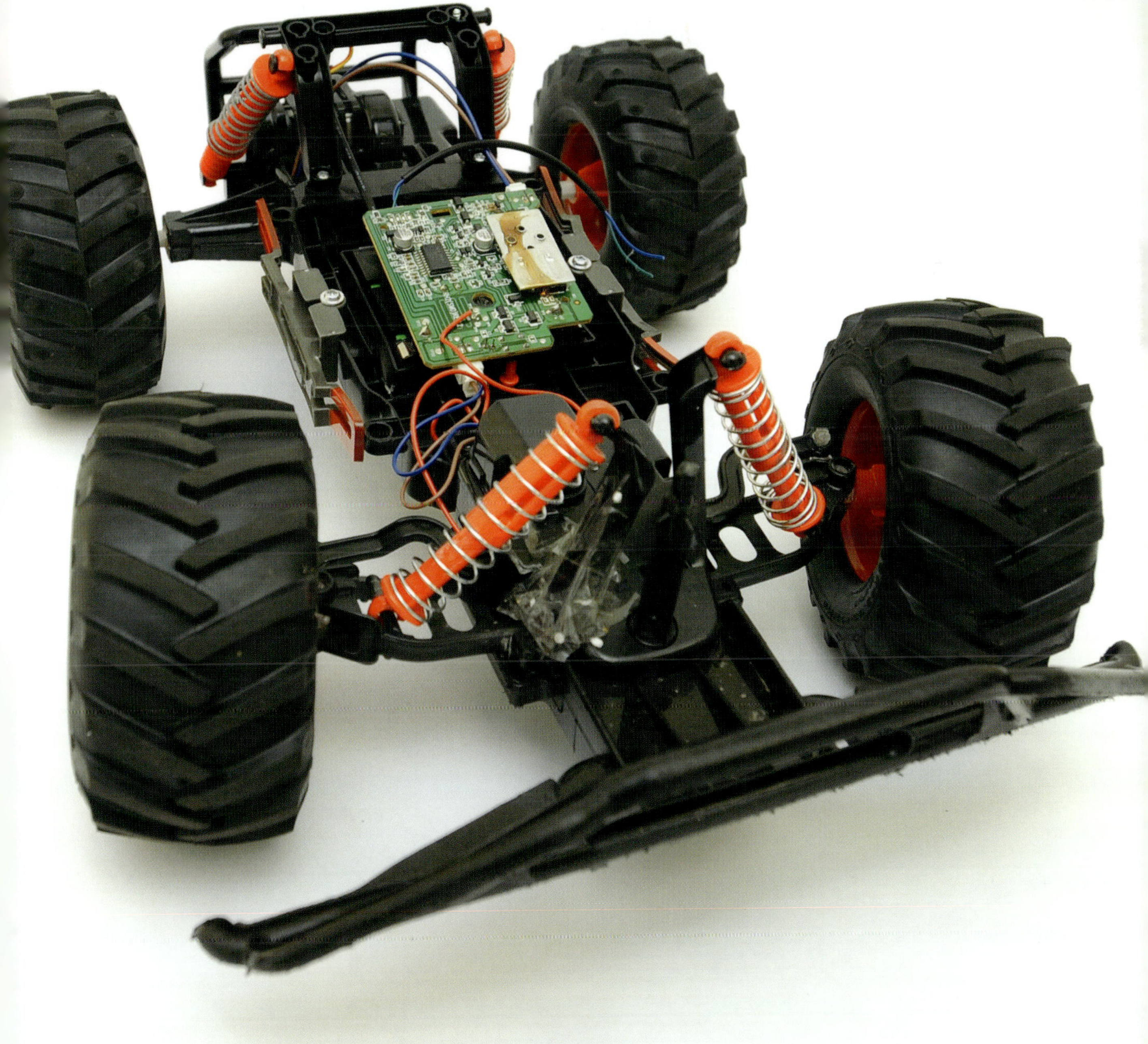

Reusing a Remote-Controlled Car

We took apart a remote-controlled car and learned what was inside. Now what? Here are some ideas for how to reuse the parts of a remote-controlled car. Can you think of any more?

- **Wheel Swap:** Try swapping the wheels with the wheels of another car. Can you turn a regular car into a monster truck?
- **Modify Your Car:** Take parts off the car, then think about how this might make it drive differently. For example, how would taking off the shock absorbers change things?

Glossary

antenna (an-TEN-uh): An antenna is a wire that sends or receives radio signals. An antenna in the remote sends signals, and an antenna in the car receives them.

circuit board (SUR-kit BORD): A circuit board is a piece of material that holds computer chips, switches, and other parts. The remote-controlled car and the remote both contain a circuit board.

delicate (DEL-uh-kuht) Something is delicate if it can be broken easily. The parts inside a remote-controlled car are delicate.

motors (MOH-turz): Motors are the parts of machines that create motion. Motors allow the remote-controlled car to move forward and steer.

radio signal (RAY-dee-oh SIG-nuhl): A radio signal is a wave of invisible energy that can carry information. The remote control uses a radio signal to tell the car what to do.

To Learn More

IN THE LIBRARY

Hatton, Thomas. *Remote-Control Cars.* New York, NY: Cavendish Square, 2014.

Holzweiss, Kristina. *Amazing Makerspace DIY with Electricity*. New York, NY: Scholastic, 2018.

Pettiford, Rebecca. *Hybrid and Electric Cars.* Minneapolis, MN: Jump!, 2017.

ON THE WEB

Visit our website for links about taking apart a remote-controlled car: **childsworld.com/links**

Note to Parents, Teachers, and Librarians: We routinely verify our Web links to make sure they are safe and active sites. So encourage your readers to check them out!

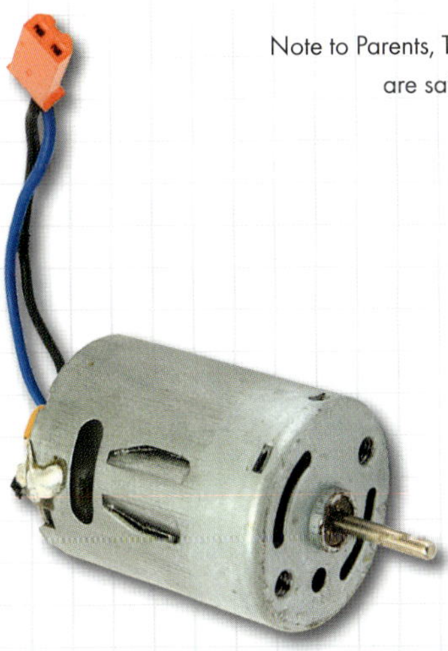

Index